STUDY GUIDE

The Parables of Jesus

R.C. Sproul

LIGONIER MINISTRIES
Renew your Mind.
LIGONIER.ORG | 800-435-4343

421 Ligonier Court, Sanford, FL 32771
Email: info@ligonier.org

Printed in China.

1

Introduction to the Parables of Jesus

MESSAGE INTRODUCTION

When Jesus Christ came to earth, He did not simply arrive on a Thursday, die on a Friday, and rise on a Sunday. Rather, He lived for over thirty years as a full-fledged member of the human race. His earthly ministry is significant for a number of reasons, especially for His prolific teaching about the kingdom of God. In fact, many people who reject the Christian faith still have great respect for Jesus as a wise, virtuous, and gifted teacher. In this series, Dr. R.C. Sproul will explore the teaching ministry of Jesus, focusing particularly on eleven of His parables. During our time together we will discuss why Jesus was such a gifted teacher, and we will seek a greater understanding and affection for the significant and timeless message that He proclaimed.

SCRIPTURE READINGS

Matthew 13:34-35; Matthew 22:16; Mark 1:21-28; Luke 4:31-32; John 12:49

TEACHING OBJECTIVES

1. To present Jesus Christ as history's greatest teacher and communicator.
2. To describe the role of parables in the Bible.
3. To explain Jesus' purposes for teaching in parables.
4. To discuss the elements of salvation and judgment within the ministry and mission of Jesus.

QUOTATIONS

Our Saviour's parables are distinguished above all others for clearness, purity, chasteness, intelligibility, importance of instruction, and simplicity. They are taken mostly from the affairs of common life, and intelligible, therefore, to all men. They contain much of himself: his doctrine, life, design in coming, and claims; and are therefore of importance to all men; and they are told in a style of native simplicity intelligible to the child, yet instructive to men of every rank and age. In his parables, as in all his instructions, he excelled all men in the purity, importance, and sublimity of his doctrine.

–Albert Barnes

He stood in the midst of Scribes and Pharisees, publicans and sinners, and preached the glad tidings...His preaching was full of parables, plain to those who had understanding, but often dark and mysterious even to His own followers, for it was a judgment from the Lord upon that evil generation that seeing they should not see and hearing they should not perceive.

–Charles Spurgeon

LECTURE OUTLINE

I. Jesus the Teacher
  - A. Jesus Christ was the greatest teacher who ever lived.
    - i. Jesus is the very incarnation of truth.
    - ii. The content of Jesus' teaching is impeccable and of divine origin.
    - iii. He was a master pedagogue with an extraordinary style of teaching.
  - B. Jesus' contemporaries recognized His unique teaching abilities.
    - i. "No one ever spoke like this man!" (John 7:46)
    - ii. "And when Jesus finished these sayings, the crowds were astonished at his teaching, for he was teaching them as one who had authority, and not as their scribes." (Matthew 7:28-29)
  - C. Jesus taught with a unique authority.
    - i. The Greek word for authority is *exousia*.
      1. The prefix *ex-* means "from" or "out of" (exit, exodus).
      2. The word *ousia* is a present participle of the word "to be," and it can be translated as "being," "essence," or "substance."
    - ii. Because Jesus taught with *exousia*, His teaching is not frivolous, but carries weight and substance.
    - iii. Jesus taught with the unique authority of God Himself. (John 12:49)

II. The Significance of Parables
  - A. Though Jesus used parables in a unique way, He was not the only one to use them.
    - i. Parables played a role in the traditions and teachings of the rabbis in Jesus' day.
    - ii. The Pharisees used parables to explain or illustrate the meaning of the Mosaic Law of the Old Testament.
    - iii. Jesus did not simply use parables to illustrate previous revelation; He used them to give new revelation.
  - B. Though parables are rare in the Old Testament, they are still significant.

  i. After David's sin with Bathsheba, the prophet Nathan confronted the king with a parable.
  ii. David responded to the parable with outrage, not realizing that he himself was the perpetrator of the crime in the parable.
  iii. Nathan's parable was an effective teaching tool in a moment of crisis.

C. Parables can clarify the meaning of what is being said.
  i. The English word "parable" comes from the Greek word *parabolē*.
    1. The prefix *para-* describes something that functions alongside something else (para-church, paralegal).
    2. The word *bolē* refers to something that is thrown or hurled.
  ii. A parable, then, is thrown alongside other teaching in order to illustrate a concept or clarify meaning.
  iii. Similarly, preachers will use stories and illustrations to heighten the listener's ability to understand what is being said.

D. Parables can conceal the meaning of what is being said.
  i. Jesus concluded the parable of the sower with "He who has ears to hear, let him hear." (Mark 4:9)
  ii. Jesus beckons his listeners not just to hear the sounds that are being made, but to understand and embrace his teaching.
  iii. The Greek word for obedience is *hupakouē*, which includes *akouē*, the word for hearing.
  iv. Obedience, then, is a deliberate act of hearing and heeding an instruction or command.
  v. Jesus' parables penetrate the hearts and minds of some people but not others.
    1. To those who have ears to hear, parables bring a deeper understanding of the things of God.
    2. To those who do not have ears to hear, parables are instruments of concealing and obscuring the mystery of the kingdom of God.

III. The Crisis of Jesus' Ministry

A. By nature, fallen human beings have no desire to hear or understand God's words.

B. God's words, then, bring salvation for those who believe and judgment for those who do not.
  i. In Isaiah 6, God commissioned Isaiah to shut the people's eyes, stop up their ears, and harden their hearts.
  ii. Though most will be given over to their sinful desires and will be judged, God will preserve a remnant.

C. In the New Testament, Jesus' entrance into the world is sometimes described by the word *krisis*.

D. *Krisis* refers to judgment and is the root of the English word "crisis."

E. Christ's coming is good news for some and bad news for others.
  i. Jesus causes some to rise and others to fall.

   ii. He has not brought peace, but a sword. (Matthew 10:34-35)
   iii. Christ is both the cornerstone of the church and a stumbling stone for unbelievers.
   iv. Jesus is the aroma of salvation for those who love Him, and He is the grounds of condemnation for those who oppose Him.

F. Jesus' use of parables reflects his two-fold mission of salvation and judgment.

STUDY QUESTIONS

1. Which of the following is *not* a reason for considering Jesus the greatest teacher who lived?
   a. He is a master pedagogue with an extraordinary teaching style.
   b. He invented the parable as a new way to reveal divine truth.
   c. He is the incarnation of truth.
   d. His teaching had a divine origin.

2. Jesus used parables not just to explain previous revelation, but to give new revelation.
   a. True
   b. False

3. Jesus is the only person in the Bible to use parables.
   a. True
   b. False

4. In the New Testament, the function of parables is ___________.
   a. To explain truths about the kingdom of God.
   b. To obscure and conceal truths about the kingdom of God.
   c. To illustrate and clarify the teachings of Jesus.
   d. All of the above.

5. In Isaiah 6:8-10, what was God's purpose for Isaiah's ministry?
   a. That the people of Israel would repent and follow God's ways
   b. That Isaiah would destroy the idols in the land
   c. That Isaiah would lead Israel to victory against its enemies
   d. That the Israelites would harden their hearts and be judged

BIBLE STUDY AND DISCUSSION QUESTIONS

1. Why was Jesus a great teacher? What characteristics set his teaching apart from that of the other religious leaders in his day?

2. Which parable of Jesus has been particularly meaningful to you? How has God used this parable in your life? With which parable do you wrestle the most?

3. When Jesus said, "He who has ears to hear, let him hear" in Mark 4:9, what did He mean? How does this verse shed light on the purpose of parables within the teaching ministry of Jesus?

4. In what ways does Jesus bring good news? In what ways does He bring bad news? How does this two-fold reality affect the church's proclamation of the gospel?

2

Parable of the Unjust Judge

MESSAGE INTRODUCTION

In a fallen world, corruption and oppression are not strangers, even to Christians. Sadly, those who profess faith in Christ sometimes participate in corrupt and oppressive practices. At other times, Christians may find themselves to be the objects of exploitation, persecution, and scorn. Though it can be tempting to give in to despair or to lash out in anger, God calls his people to respond prayerfully in all circumstances. In this lecture Dr. Sproul will examine the parable of the unjust judge, which reveals God to be the great Refuge and Advocate of those who are in need.

SCRIPTURE READINGS

Luke 18:1-8

TEACHING OBJECTIVES

1. To describe the differences between allegorical and non-allegorical approaches to interpreting the parables of Jesus.
2. To present and exegete the parable of the unjust judge in Luke 18:1-8.
3. To promote a spirit of persistence in prayer among Christ's followers.
4. To encourage believers to look to God for deliverance and hope in the midst of their trials.

QUOTATIONS

It is not right to search curiously, and word by word, into all things in a parable; but when we have learned the object for which it was composed, we are to reap this, and not to busy ourselves about anything further.

–John Chrysostom

We know that perseverance in prayer is a rare and difficult attainment; and it is a manifestation of our unbelief that, when our first prayers are not successful, we immediately throw away not only hope, but all the ardor of prayer. But it is an undoubted evidence of our faith, if we are disappointed of our wish, and yet do not lose courage. Most properly, therefore, does Christ recommend to his disciples to persevere in praying.

–John Calvin

We ought to concern ourselves for the persecuted and oppressed churches, and to pray that God would do them justice, and set them in safety. And herein we must be very urgent; we must cry with earnestness: we must cry day and night, as those that believe prayer will be heard at last; we must wrestle with God, as those that know how to value the blessing, and will have no nay. God's praying people are told to give him no rest.

–Matthew Henry

LECTURE OUTLINE

I. Interpretive Approaches
   A. In the early centuries of Christianity, the church fathers employed the allegorical method of interpretation.
      i. They applied this method both to parables and to the entire Bible.
      ii. This approach looks for hidden meaning in each element of the parable.
      iii. This method is similar to the allegory of *Pilgrim's Progress*, in which each character illustrates a particular truth or represents a specific type of person.
   B. In recent centuries, most scholars have come to agree that each parable has a central decisive point.
      i. Rather than each character demonstrating a different principle, they all combine to present a single message.
      ii. A few of the more complex parables may have two or three major points, but most have only one.
      iii. This approach avoids the allegorizing tendency to find hidden significance in every element of the story, which can lead to misinterpretation and confusion.
      iv. The task at hand, therefore, is to discover the single important central point of the parable.

II. The Value of Perseverance
   A. Some of Winston Churchill's most memorable and provocative speeches were exhortations to persevere through hardship.
      i. When Churchill had been invited to speak at his alma mater, he addressed the students with the words "Never, ever give up!"
      ii. Throughout his time in office, Churchill sought to instill within the English people an indomitable spirit of fidelity and perseverance.

B. At the outset, Luke reveals the goal of the parable of the unjust judge.
   i. Jesus tells this parable so that the listeners "ought always to pray and not lose heart." (Luke 18:1)
   ii. This parable focuses on persistent prayer in the midst of difficulty and trouble.

III. The Widow and the Judge

A. In order to communicate the truth of constant prayer, Jesus tells the story of a widow who had no one to vindicate her against her adversary.
B. In Scripture, widows occupy a special place in the heart of God.
   i. Widows are among the most vulnerable in society, both then and now.
   ii. The essence of true religion is caring for widows and orphans. (James 1:27)
   iii. In this parable, Jesus tells the story of a widow who had been treated unjustly, and whose only hope was to find justice at the hands of the judge.
C. In this story, the widow went to plead her case before a judge who does not fear God nor regard man.
   i. Since this judge did not care about God or people, he did not care about justice.
   ii. In television and popular culture, we often see depictions of trials where close attention is paid to legal precedents and the finer points of the law, but in which the fundamental question of justice is lost.
   iii. Sadly, many judges and officials, both then and today, care chiefly about their own office, prestige, and job security.

IV. The Widow's Persistence

A. When the widow sought the judge's help, he refused to help her.
B. Even when the judge refused to help her a second time, she would not take "no" for an answer.
C. Because the widow kept coming back, the judge finally grew weary and granted her request.
   i. The woman was importunate, which means "extremely persistent."
   ii. Although the judge did not care about justice, her persistence led him to support her cause.

V. God's Justice and Faithfulness

A. This parable, like many others, reveals a contrast between how fallen creatures behave and how God behaves.
   i. This contrast is often expressed by the phrases "How much more...?" and "Will not God...?"
   ii. In this passage Jesus asks, "And will not God give justice to His elect, who cry to Him day and night?"

   iii. Unlike the judge in the parable, God cares deeply about his people and will grant them justice.

B. Although God's people are often exploited and treated unjustly, they are not to seek vengeance upon evildoers.
   i. "Vengeance is mine, I will repay," says the Lord. (Romans 12:19)
   ii. God will right the wrongs that His people have experienced.
   iii. In the book of Exodus, God reveals Himself as the one who hears the suffering of His people and liberates them from bondage.

C. God has promised to defend and vindicate His people.
   i. The exodus from Egypt is a foretaste of the greater exodus in the New Testament, when God delivers His people from the world, the flesh, and the devil.
   ii. When Christians are reviled and persecuted for their faith, Christ, who declares them to be blessed, will vindicate them. (Matthew 5:10-12)
   iii. Even though we may not think God hears our prayers, God knows us intimately and will intervene for our good and for His glory.
   iv. Because we serve a God who hears us and cares about us, we are to persevere in prayer and not lose heart.
   v. When Christ returns, He will find faith on earth because He is faithful to keep and preserve those whom the Father has given to Him.

STUDY QUESTIONS

1. The allegorical method of interpretation ___________.
   a. Searches for hidden meaning in each element of a parable
   b. Was employed by most of the ancient church fathers
   c. Can be applied both to the entire Bible and to parables specifically
   d. All of the above
   e. A and B only

2. According to Dr. Sproul, a parable will never have more than one point.
   a. True
   b. False

3. James 1:27 reminds Christians that pure and undefiled religion finds expression in caring for ___________, who are among the most vulnerable people in society.
   a. Religious leaders
   b. Widows and orphans
   c. Rulers and authority figures
   d. Enemies and persecutors

4. How does the judge in Luke 18:1-8 relate to God?
   a. The judge repented of his sin, showing God's mercy toward sinners.
   b. The judge's kindness toward the widow is an analogy for God's kindness toward those who are in need.
   c. The judge's decision to help the widow reveals God's power to change the hearts of oppressors.
   d. Jesus contrasts the unjust and apathetic judge with the faithful God who vindicates His people.

5. Although God's people are sometimes reviled, exploited and treated unjustly, they are not to seek vengeance upon evildoers.
   a. True
   b. False

BIBLE STUDY AND DISCUSSION QUESTIONS

1. Why do Christians need to be reminded and encouraged to be persistent in prayer? What are some reasons why Christians might lose heart and give in to despair? Why is it significant that Jesus told a parable to encourage Christians to pray persistently?

2. Describe the widow's situation in Luke 18:3. How did the judge respond to the widow? How does the judge's response to the widow compare to God's response to His people who are in need?

3. What does "importunate" mean? What does it mean to be importunate in prayer?

4. At first glance, Luke 18:7-8, may appear to imply that God will always furnish swift and satisfactory answers to the prayers of His people. How should these verses be understood? Should Christians lose heart when God does not seem to be answering our prayers? Explain your answer.

3

Parable of the Rich Fool

MESSAGE INTRODUCTION

Material prosperity can bring with it significant spiritual dangers. Sadly, many people who have enjoyed a comfortable standard of living find themselves neglecting God and neighbor in the quest for comfort and riches. Some seek security from money and possessions instead of from God, making an idol out of the good things that God provides. Others, driven by greed, resort to unethical and corrupt means of pursuing personal gain. In the midst of these pitfalls and temptations, the parable of the rich fool in Luke 12 offers a powerful reminder that fellowship with God is a far greater treasure than material wealth and personal belongings.

SCRIPTURE READINGS

Luke 12:13-21

TEACHING OBJECTIVES

1. To present and exegete the parable of the rich fool in Luke 12:13-21.
2. To discuss the potent dangers of covetousness, both then and today.
3. To warn against the ways that the desire for personal gain can undermine love for God and for other people.
4. To encourage believers to examine their own hearts and pursue God as their greatest treasure.

QUOTATIONS

Christ first guards his followers against covetousness, and next, in order to cure their minds entirely of this disease, he declares, that our life consisteth not in abundance. These words point out the inward fountain and source, from which flows the mad eagerness for gain. It is because the general belief is, that a man is happy in proportion as he possesses much, and that the happiness of life is produced by riches. Hence arise those immoderate desires, which, like a fiery furnace, send forth their flames, and yet cease not to burn within.

–John Calvin

Therefore, you preachers, out with your swords and strike at the root. Speak against covetousness, and cry out upon it. Stand not ticking and toying at the branches nor at the boughs, for then there will new boughs and branches spring again of them; but strike at the root, and fear not these giants of England, these great men and men of power, these men that are oppressors of the poor; fear them not, but strike at the root of all evil, which is mischievous covetousness.

–Hugh Latimer

LECTURE OUTLINE

I. Setting
  A. Jesus had been asked to arbitrate a dispute over inheritance.
    i. According to Jewish law, inheritance disputes could be settled by a rabbi.
    ii. In addition to being a teacher, a rabbi could also serve as an attorney or legal arbitrator.
  B. In this case, the young man wanted Jesus to represent his vested interests.
    i. This man was not interested in what Jesus had to say, but in what Jesus could do for him.
    ii. For this man, Jesus represented an opportunity for financial gain.
  C. Jesus responded with a warning against covetousness.
    i. Most people today probably do not regard coveting as wrong or dangerous.
    ii. Significantly, in the Ten Commandments, God gave His people a law against coveting.
    iii. Greed and jealousy can be the precursors to war, theft, violence, dishonesty, and slander.
  D. Jesus told a parable to communicate the danger of covetousness.

II. The Abundance of the Rich Man
  A. The rich man's land produced a plentiful harvest, and he did not have room to store all his crops.
    i. This man was wealthy because of what the ground had produced.
    ii. Ultimately, this man was not rich because of his own toil, but because of God's providential blessing.
    iii. Every good and perfect gift comes from the Father. (James 1:17)
  B. The rich man did not recognize God as the source of his prosperity.
    i. Among the most basic of human sins are the refusal to honor God as God and the refusal to be grateful to Him.

   ii. The New Testament consistently promotes a posture of thanksgiving before God. (Ephesians 5:4; Philippians 4:6; Colossians 2:7; 2 Thessalonians 1:3)
   iii. By addressing God in a spirit of thanksgiving, we acknowledge that we are not self-sufficient but are recipients of His mercy and grace.

III. The Self-Absorption of the Rich Man
- A. Although he had more than he needed, the rich man's main priority was hoarding and preserving his wealth.
   - i. He did not seek ways of enriching his neighbors or his community.
   - ii. Instead, he decided to tear down his barns and build bigger ones.
- B. The rich man did not follow the Old Testament law of returning the firstfruits of his harvest to God.
   - i. In contemporary terms, he did not consider giving a tithe of his riches to God.
   - ii. As one of the Old Testament's moral commandments, the obligation to tithe has not been nullified by the New Testament.
   - iii. Like many Christians today, this man obsessed over his possessions to the extent that he did not give God what was rightfully His.
   - iv. Professing Christians who refuse to tithe ought to examine their hearts to see if they share the rich man's unbelief.

IV. The Folly of the Rich Man
- A. This man is described not only as wealthy, but also as a fool.
   - i. In biblical categories, a fool is not someone who is unintelligent or uneducated.
   - ii. In fact, Aristotle observed that there is a foolish corner in the mind of even the most brilliant man.
- B. To be called a fool is a moral judgment.
   - i. It is the fool who says in his heart, "There is no God." (Psalm 14:1)
   - ii. In the midst of his success, the rich fool ignored God and only took his own interests into account.
   - iii. This man lived as if God did not exist and as if all that mattered was pleasure and momentary gratification.
   - iv. Folly is the antithesis of wisdom, which begins with the fear of the Lord. (Proverbs 1:7)
- C. While this man was celebrating, God brought the accusation of folly against him.
   - i. That very night, the rich fool's soul was demanded of him.
   - ii. God was not impressed or satisfied with the rich man's wealth and possessions.
   - iii. Sadly, though he was rich in treasures, this man was not rich toward God and was not prepared to meet the Lord.

STUDY QUESTIONS

1. The parable of the rich fool primarily addresses the sin of __________.
   a. Indifference to the poor
   b. Slothfulness
   c. Covetousness
   d. Corruption

2. Although the rich man's wealth came from God, he did not give God thanks or praise.
   a. True
   b. False

3. What was the rich man's solution to the problem of having insufficient space to store his crops?
   a. He decided to tear down his barns and build bigger ones.
   b. He gave a portion of his harvest to the poor and needy.
   c. He sold the surplus crops and buried the money in the ground.
   d. He offered the firstfruits of his crops to God and hoarded the rest.

4. As one of the Old Testament's civil commandments, the obligation to tithe has been nullified by the New Testament.
   a. True
   b. False

5. In biblical categories, a fool is __________.
   a. Unintelligent
   b. One who lives as if there is no God
   c. Culturally backwards
   d. Uneducated and ignorant about the basic workings of life

BIBLE STUDY AND DISCUSSION QUESTIONS

1. The man who approached Jesus in Luke 12:13 was not interested in hearing Jesus teach. Instead, he wanted to use Jesus for his own personal gain. In what ways do Christians reveal this attitude toward Jesus today? How have you been tempted to use or recruit Jesus for your own purposes?

2. What is covetousness? Why is it wrong? What other sins can come as a result of a covetous spirit?

3. Jesus reminds us in Luke 13:15 that "one's life does not consist in the abundance of his possessions." All material blessings come from God and belong to God. This parable warns against the danger of storing up earthly treasures while being impoverished in the things of God. How does this parable apply to the way we manage God's money with regard to 1) tithing? 2) giving to the poor and needy? 3) planning for the future?

4. What is a biblical definition of a fool? What are some ways that you are tempted to live as if God did not exist? How might God be calling you to repent and change?

4

Parable of the Rich Man and Lazarus

MESSAGE INTRODUCTION

As creatures who have rebelled against a holy God, we have become thoroughly ensnared to the power of sin. In this fallen state, we pursue our own interests and desires with little regard for God or others. Sadly, our contempt for our holy Creator often prompts us to treat His image-bearers with injustice and indifference. In Luke 16:19-31, Jesus tells a striking parable about a rich man and a beggar named Lazarus. This parable reveals both the extent of human sin and the dire eternal consequences that await those who do not turn to Jesus in repentance for their sins.

SCRIPTURE READINGS

Luke 16:19-31

TEACHING OBJECTIVES

1. To present and exegete the parable of the rich man and Lazarus in Luke 16:19-31.
2. To highlight the connection between our relationship with God and the way we treat those who are less fortunate than we are.
3. To discuss the grave and eternal consequences for human sin against a holy and just God.
4. To exalt Jesus as the only one who can liberate us from the power and presence of sin.
5. To remind Christians of their responsibility to share the gospel of Jesus Christ with those who have not yet believed.

QUOTATIONS

In the person of Lazarus there is held out to us a striking proof that we ought not to pronounce men to be accursed by God, because they drag out, in incessant pain, a life which is full of distresses. In him the grace of God was so entirely hidden, and buried by the deformity and shame of the cross, that to the eye of the flesh nothing presented itself except the curse; and yet we see that in a body which was loathsome and full of rottenness there was lodged a soul unspeakably precious, which is carried by angels to a blessed life.

–John Calvin

Human ingenuity has done very much to bridge great gulfs. Scarcely has the world afforded a river so wide that its floods could not be leaped over, or a torrent so furious that it could not be made to pass under the yoke. High above the foam of Columbia's glorious waterfall, man has hung aloft his slender, but substantial road of iron—and the shriek of the locomotive is heard above the roar of Niagara...There is, however, one gulf which no human skill or engineering ever shall be able to bridge. There is one chasm which no wing shall ever be able to cross. It is the gulf which divides the world of joy, in which the righteous triumph, from that land of sorrow in which the wicked feel the smart of Jehovah's sword.

–Charles Spurgeon

LECTURE OUTLINE

I. Contrasting Lives
   A. The rich man enjoyed an opulent lifestyle.
      i. He dressed like royalty, in purple and fine linen.
      ii. He feasted sumptuously on a daily basis.
   B. In contrast, Lazarus was an impoverished beggar.
      i. He was afflicted with a chronic skin disease that left his body covered with sores.
      ii. Unable to move himself, he had to be carried to the gate of the rich man's home.
      iii. In his state of hunger, Lazarus was eager to eat the crumbs that fell from the rich man's table.
   C. Dogs offered Lazarus the kindness that the rich man would not give.
      i. In first-century Jewish culture, dogs were seen as unclean, scavenging beasts.
      ii. As Lazarus lay at the rich man's gate, dogs came and licked his wounds.
      iii. The dogs gave Lazarus the same healing treatment that they would give to themselves if they were injured.
      iv. Even the unclean dogs had a higher regard for human life than the rich man did.

II. Contrasting Deaths
   A. When Lazarus died, angels carried him to Abraham's side.
      i. Nothing is said of his burial, and there is no evidence that his death really mattered to anyone.
      ii. However, incomprehensible honor and glory awaited him after his death.
   B. When the rich man died, he experienced torment in Hades.
      i. Luke mentions the burial that the rich man received.
      ii. However, he did not receive any heavenly honors.
      iii. Even in his torment, he did not cry out to God in repentance.

III. Contrasting Eternities
   A. As the rich man was in Hades, he looked up and saw Lazarus at Abraham's side.
   B. Instead of crying out to God, the rich man asked Abraham to ameliorate his condition of suffering.
      i. Still regarding Lazarus as a lowly beggar, he asked Abraham to send him as a servant to cool his tongue with water.
      ii. The man who once feasted sumptuously was now begging desperately for a drop of water.
   C. Abraham denied the rich man's request.
      i. During his life, the rich man enjoyed every comfort that Lazarus had lacked.
      ii. In a twist of poetic justice, their situations were now reversed.

IV. The Grave Reality of Eternal Punishment
   A. There is no way to cross over from one eternal destination to the other.
      i. Lazarus could not come to the rich man's relief because there was a great chasm separating Hades from the bosom of Abraham.
      ii. After his death, it was too late for the rich man to turn from his wicked ways and avoid the grim consequences of his sin.
      iii. Although he had been given numerous second chances throughout his life, he did not repent or turn from his self-absorbed lifestyle.
   B. Jesus frequently warned people about the reality of eternal judgment.
      i. In the Gospels, Jesus taught more about hell than heaven.
      ii. Jesus taught that on the day of judgment people will be called to give an account for every careless or idle word they have spoken.
   C. Fallen humans need a change of heart in order to be awakened to their state of spiritual peril.
      i. The rich man asked for Lazarus to be sent to warn his five brothers so that they would not have to experience eternal torment.
      ii. Because the brothers already had the Old Testament writings, it would accomplish nothing to send Lazarus to warn them.
      iii. If their hearts were hardened against the warnings in Moses and the Prophets, the brothers would not repent even if someone were to rise from the dead and speak to them.

D. In the same way, those among Jesus' listeners whose hearts were hardened toward God's Word would refuse to repent and believe even after Jesus was raised from the dead.
   i. The warning is clear: now is the time to repent and to seal our eternal state.
   ii. Once we die, it is too late.
   iii. While change is still possible, we must ask God to open our eyes to the life-changing truths of Scripture, that we might repent and believe the good news of Jesus Christ.

STUDY QUESTIONS

1. Why is it significant that the dog licked Lazarus' wounds?
   a. Even unclean animals exceeded the rich man in compassion.
   b. Lazarus died of an infection contracted from the unclean dogs.
   c. The dogs added to Lazarus' earthly misery by licking his wounds.
   d. The rich man was so cruel that the dogs preferred the ill Lazarus.

2. The rich man did not cry out to God in repentance until after he began to experience torment in Hades.
   a. True
   b. False

3. After their situations were reversed, the rich man regarded Lazarus as ____________.
   a. A man of wisdom and integrity.
   b. A beggar and servant, just like before.
   c. The more spiritually mature of the two men.
   d. Someone to whom he should have been more generous.

4. During His earthly ministry, Jesus taught less about heaven than He did about hell.
   a. True
   b. False

5. According to the parable, if Lazarus had been raised from the dead to warn the rich man's brothers about eternal judgment, how would they have responded?
   a. They would have believed his message.
   b. Lazarus' message would have led them to search the Scriptures.
   c. If they already ignored Scripture, they would ignore Lazarus also.
   d. Some brothers would have believed Lazarus, but others would not.

BIBLE STUDY AND DISCUSSION QUESTIONS

1. The rich man in this parable was not condemned for being wealthy. Rather, his indifference toward Lazarus was a symptom of a deeper spiritual problem (see Proverbs 14:31 and 17:5). What do the rich man's attitude and actions reveal about his relationship with God?

2. As mentioned above, one way to measure a person's spiritual heartbeat is by looking at that person's outlook toward those who are in need. Consider your own attitude and conduct toward the destitute and disadvantaged; what do they indicate about your view of Who God is? How might there be a disconnect between what you profess about God and how you respond to His image-bearers?

3. In today's world, it has become increasingly unpopular and controversial to speak of a doctrine of eternal punishment. What does Luke 16:19-31 say about the eternal state of those who reject God? What questions about the future does this passage leave unanswered?

4. The doctrine of hell reminds Christians of our calling to proclaim the gospel to unbelievers. What does this parable say about the urgency of sharing the good news with others? See Luke 16:31. What, instead of miraculous signs, are our greatest assets when we tell people about Jesus?

5

Parable of the Hidden Treasure & Parable of the Pearl of Great Price

MESSAGE INTRODUCTION

When the apostle Paul reflected on his life experiences, he observed that his greatest human accomplishments were like rubbish compared to the surpassing worth of knowing Jesus Christ (Philippians 3:7-9). Even though he had much to be proud of, Paul willingly gave it all up so that he might know Christ and be found in Him. Although the parables of the hidden treasure and the pearl of great price are some of the shortest parables of Jesus, their rich imagery powerfully expresses what Paul learned to be true, that Jesus Christ is the greatest treasure that any person could ever hope to attain.

SCRIPTURE READINGS

Matthew 13:44-46

TEACHING OBJECTIVES

1. To present and exegete the parable of the hidden treasure and the parable of the pearl of great price in Matthew 13:44-46.
2. To examine subjective and objective ideas of value.
3. To discuss the need for fallen humans to value the things that God values.
4. To exalt Jesus Christ as supremely valuable, worthy of abandoning all for the sake of receiving Him.

QUOTATIONS

Those who would have a saving interest in Christ must be willing to part with all for him, leave all to follow him. Whatever stands in opposition to Christ, or in competition with him for our love and service, we must cheerfully quit it, though ever so dear to us.

–Matthew Henry

We see, in this simple picture, the conduct of a true Christian explained. He is what he is, and does what he does in his religion, because he is thoroughly persuaded that it is worthwhile. He comes out from the world; he puts off the old man; he forsakes the vain companions of his past life. Like Matthew, he gives up everything, and like Paul, he counts "all things loss" for Christ's sake. And why? Because he is convinced that Christ will make amends to him for all he gives up. He sees in Christ an endless "treasure," he sees in Christ a precious "pearl": to win Christ he will make any sacrifice. This is true faith. This is the stamp of a genuine work of the Holy Ghost.

–J.C. Ryle

LECTURE OUTLINE

I. The Question of Value
   A. The parables of the hidden treasure and the pearl of great price both deal with the value of the kingdom of heaven.
   B. In contemporary usage, the concept of value or values is sometimes used as a synonym for ethics.
      i. Political discussions often allude to "national values" or "family values."
      ii. In these instances, such "values" normally refer to objective moral standards.
   C. Strictly speaking, however, value has to do with an individual's subjective appraisal of something's worth.
      i. A car might be of greater value in the eyes of its current owner than it is in the eyes of a potential buyer.
      ii. Money is a frequent source of marital tension when a husband and wife value things differently.
   D. When values and ethics converge, we see that our value systems do not always agree with God's value system.
      i. As Christians, we have an imperative to bring our personal values into line with the values that God assigns to things.
      ii. When Jesus announced that the kingdom of heaven had arrived, he announced something of inestimable value to people who did not place a high value on it.

II. The Pursuit of Treasure

A. Many popular stories are about treasure hunts.
  i. Pirates or outlaws will conceal a hoard of treasure and make a map to help them find it at a later time.
  ii. Years later, others will find the map and try to recover the lost treasure.

B. In this parable, a worker unexpectedly came across treasure that had been buried in a field.
  i. In the ancient world, it was not uncommon for people to bury valuable items for safekeeping.
  ii. If the owner died before returning to the treasure, it would remain concealed in the ground until someone else happened to find it.

C. When this worker found the treasure, he decided to sell all of his belongings in order to purchase the field that contained the buried valuables.
  i. His one burning passion was to acquire the treasure.
  ii. Once he owned the field, the treasure was his also.

D. In the same way, a jewelry merchant came across the finest pearl that he had ever seen.
  i. His collection would have included many valuable pearls and gems.
  ii. He parted with his entire collection in order to purchase the pearl of great price.

E. In these parables, both men came across something so valuable that they would gladly sacrifice everything else in order to possess it.

III. God's Values and Ours

A. In a typical economic exchange, both parties profit.
  i. The seller is paid for his wares.
  ii. The buyer exchanges his money for an item that is more important to him than the money he pays to obtain it.

B. Jesus asked his listeners how much a human soul is worth.
  i. "What shall a man give in return for his soul?" (Matthew 16:26)
  ii. Certain literary works have explored the idea of a person selling his soul to the devil in exchange for particular powers or pleasures.
  iii. For the Christian, salvation has too high a value to be exchanged for anything.

C. In the value system of God, the kingdom of heaven surpasses every other item or treasure in worth.
  i. We ought to examine our value systems and align them with the things that God values.
  ii. We are to pursue what Jesus pursues and resist what Jesus resists.
  iii. We should be prepared to sacrifice everything in order to possess Christ.

STUDY QUESTIONS

1. Value, in its most basic sense, describes ___________.
   a. A social cause often associated with a political platform.
   b. An individual's subjective appraisal of something's worth.
   c. A good or service that is available at a competitive price.
   d. An objective moral principle.

2. Christians are called to align their personal value systems with the values of God.
   a. True
   b. False

3. In ancient Hebrew culture, ___________ was a common method of safeguarding valuable possessions.
   a. Concealing or burying goods.
   b. Hiring personal guards.
   c. Locking treasures in a fortified vault.
   d. Obtaining a writ of protection from the local authorities.

4. When a person purchased a field, ancient Jewish law required him to return valuable objects found within the field to the previous owner.
   a. True
   b. False

5. What do these parables teach about the kingdom of heaven?
   a. The kingdom of heaven demands everything a person has.
   b. The kingdom of heaven is the greatest treasure anyone can attain.
   c. Christ's followers must align their values to God's values.
   d. All of the above.

BIBLE STUDY AND DISCUSSION QUESTIONS

1. According to Dr. Sproul, what is the difference between the economic concept of value and the ethical notion of values? Why is this difference significant?
2. Why is it so often necessary for our value systems to be remade according to the things that God values? How does this process come about?
3. What are some of the things that you value most? How has your sense of value changed as a result of knowing Christ? How does He represent the fulfillment of some of these things that you value?
4. In both of these parables, the main characters sell all of their possessions in order to obtain something of greater worth. How has Jesus called upon you to make sacrifices for Him? What has been the most difficult thing for you to give up for the sake of Christ? How has He shown Himself to be faithful?

6

Parable of the Owner of the Vineyard

MESSAGE INTRODUCTION

Equality is highly prized in today's world. Many societies and governments are built upon the premise that all people are endowed with an essential dignity and equality. Yet, concepts like equality and fairness are sometimes pushed to an extreme degree. Consequently, it can be highly controversial to claim, as the Bible does, that God does not extend grace and mercy to all people in the same way. In this lecture, Dr. Sproul will examine the parable of the vineyard in Matthew 20, explaining that it is God's sovereign prerogative to have mercy on whom He will have mercy.

SCRIPTURE READINGS

Matthew 20:1-16

TEACHING OBJECTIVES

1. To present and exegete the parable of the owner of the vineyard in Matthew 20:1-16.
2. To examine the implications of God's sovereignty.
3. To differentiate between different categories of justice and non-justice.
4. To proclaim God's holiness and abundant mercy in electing undeserving sinners to salvation.

QUOTATIONS

Men have no right to complain of the bounty of God, when he honors unworthy persons by large rewards beyond what they deserve.

–John Calvin

We see one man called to repentance and faith in the beginning of his days like Timothy, and labouring in the Lord's vineyard for forty or fifty years; we see another man called "at the eleventh hour," like the thief on the cross, and plucked like a brand out of the fire—one day a hardened impenitent sinner, and the next day in paradise. And yet the whole tenor of the Gospel leads us to believe that both are equally forgiven before God.

–J.C. Ryle

LECTURE OUTLINE

I. Meaning and Application
   A. People often argue that the New Testament parables can have a multitude of meanings.
   B. However, orthodox Christianity has traditionally held that a biblical text only has one meaning, albeit with the possibility of a multitude of applications.
   C. The parable in Matthew 20:1-16 has a single meaning with many possible applications.
   D. Though traditionally called "the parable of the workers in the vineyard," this parable is really about the owner of the vineyard.

II. Justice, Grace, & Merit
   A. The parable of the owner of the vineyard deals with the weighty matters of justice, grace, and merit.
   B. Often, these terms are used in imprecise and confusing ways in contemporary discussions.
      i. Language is fluid, and over time the meaning of certain words can change significantly.
      ii. For example, the word "scan" originally meant "to examine closely" but can now mean "to glance at hastily."
   C. The term "justice" can also be used in paradoxical ways.
      i. At its best, "social justice" involves defending human rights, preventing exploitation of others, and aiding the more vulnerable members of society.
      ii. In certain Marxist contexts, "social justice" can describe coercive efforts to take from one person and give to another.

III. The Vineyard Owner and His Workers
   A. In this parable, a man who owned a vineyard went out to search for day laborers.
      i. When the grapes had ripened to the optimal point, it was imperative that they be harvested as quickly as possible.
      ii. Since the owner needed additional workers to bring in the harvest, he went to the marketplace, where laborers were waiting to be hired for the day.
   B. He hired several laborers who agreed to work in exchange for one denarius.
   C. As the work progressed, the owner decided to hire additional workers throughout the day.

  i. He returned and hired more workers at the third hour, the sixth hour, and the ninth hour.
  ii. When he went out at the eleventh hour, he saw some idle men who had not yet been hired by anyone.
  iii. He hired these men, and they worked during the final hour of the work day.

D. At the end of the day, the harvest had been completed, and the vineyard owner paid the workers their wages.
  i. Beginning with the last group, he paid each group of workers a denarius.
  ii. Those who had worked all day were outraged that they received the same wage as the workers who had only worked at the end of the day.
  iii. The owner reminded the first group of workers that they had agreed to work for one denarius and that he had honored that agreement.

IV. God's Sovereignty in Election

A. Those who profess to be Christians agree that God is sovereign.

B. The doctrine of God's sovereignty has many implications.
  i. God rules over the creation, and all of nature obeys His commands.
  ii. God has the right to give humans His law and therefore impose moral obligations upon His creatures.
  iii. God has the right to distribute grace to sinners in the way that He pleases.

C. God extends grace differently to different people.
  i. God gives grace to certain people that He does not give to others.
  ii. God called Abraham out of Chaldean paganism, but not Hammurabi.
  iii. Saul of Tarsus had done nothing to deserve salvation, but God graciously converted him on the road to Damascus.
  iv. According to His good pleasure, God chooses to give grace to some but not to all. (Romans 9:10-13)

V. Justice, Non-Justice, & Injustice

A. A person receives justice when he or she receives what is deserved.

B. A person receives non-justice when he or she does not receive what is deserved.
  i. A person who does not receive punishment that he or she deserves receives the non-justice of mercy.
  ii. A person who receives undeserved kindness or blessing receives the non-justice of grace.
  iii. A person who receives unrighteous and evil treatment that he or she does not deserve receives the non-justice of injustice.

C. When God demonstrates grace or mercy, He does not act justly, but He does not act wrongly either.
  i. There is nothing evil about God giving grace and forgiveness to sinners who do not deserve it.
  ii. There is nothing wrong about God giving just punishment to sinners who do deserve it.

iii. God is free to decide who will receive non-just grace and who will receive just punishment; no one receives injustice from Him.

VI. The Just and Generous Landowner

A. In Matthew 20:1-16, the owner of the vineyard did not treat any of his workers unjustly.
   i. Some of the workers received exactly what they had earned.
   ii. The other workers received more than they deserved.

B. The only person in this parable who received injustice was the landowner, who was unjustly slandered by the angry workers.

C. Just as the owner of the vineyard was free to be generous with his money, God has the sovereign authority to show mercy as He desires.

STUDY QUESTIONS

1. The workers who were hired at the beginning of the day agreed to be paid one denarius for a day's work.
   a. True
   b. False

2. The workers who were hired at the end of the day were paid ___________.
   a. Nothing
   b. More than the other workers
   c. Less than the other workers
   d. One denarius

3. God's control of creation, His right as lawgiver, and His distribution of grace to sinners are all displays of His ___________.
   a. Omnipresence
   b. Sovereignty
   c. Transcendence
   d. Omniscience

4. A person who is not punished for a crime that he or she committed has received justice.
   a. True
   b. False

5. In Matthew 20:1-16, the owner of the vineyard did not deal ___________ with any of his workers.
   a. Non-justly
   b. Justly
   c. Ethically
   d. Unjustly

BIBLE STUDY AND DISCUSSION QUESTIONS

1. What does it mean to say that God is sovereign? Do you struggle with this doctrine, or do you find it easy to accept? Why is this so?

2. In your own words, describe the difference between justice and non-justice. When is it desirable to receive justice? When is it desirable not to receive justice?

3. Are all forms of non-justice the same? Explain. How has God treated you non-justly?

4. Dr. Sproul reminds us that most parables only have one meaning. After reflecting on the parable of the vineyard owner, what would you say is the meaning of this parable? What are some of the possible applications that this parable can have?

7

Parable of the Pharisee and the Tax Collector

MESSAGE INTRODUCTION

For centuries, Christians have rightly understood pride to be a potent spiritual hazard. As common experience demonstrates, pride can undermine trust and stir up dissension in human relationships. Spiritual pride can take on even more deadly proportions. Obsessed with one's own pious accomplishments and good works, a person can easily lose sight of the extent of his or her own sin. As we shall see, the parable of the Pharisee and the tax collector warns against the danger of self-righteousness and exhorts us to approach God with humility, placing our ultimate trust in Christ alone.

SCRIPTURE READING

Luke 18:9-14

TEACHING OBJECTIVES

1. To present and exegete the parable of the Pharisee and the tax collector in Luke 18:9-14.
2. To warn against the spiritual dangers of pride and self-righteousness.
3. To articulate the biblical doctrines of justification and imputation.
4. To exalt God for the grace and mercy He demonstrates toward sinners.

QUOTATIONS

Believers must not come into the presence of God but with humility and abasement. No disease is more dangerous than arrogance; and yet all have it so deeply fixed in the marrow of their bones, that it can scarcely be removed or extirpated by any remedy. It is no doubt strange that men should be so mad as to venture to raise their crests against God, and to plead their own merits before him. Though men are carried away by their ambition, yet when we come into the presence of God, all presumption ought to be laid aside.

–John Calvin

It was the fault of the Pharisee that though he went up into the Temple to pray, he did not pray. There is no prayer in all that he said. It is one excellence of the publican that he went up to the Temple to pray and he did pray—there is nothing but prayer in all that he said.

–Charles Spurgeon

LECTURE OUTLINE

I. A *Corpus Permixtum*
   A. Jesus spoke about the Pharisee and the tax collector to "some who trusted in themselves that they were righteous, and treated others with contempt." (Luke 18:9)
   B. A recurring theme in Jesus' parables is the announcement of the impending crisis that comes from the inbreaking of the kingdom of God in the ministry of Jesus.
   C. Jesus repeatedly issued sober and serious warnings to those who made professions of faith but did not actually possess what they professed.
   D. The church is a *corpus permixtum*, a mixed body.
      i. The church includes both wheat and tares. (Matthew 13:24-30)
      ii. The church includes both true believers and those who make professions of faith without having authentic faith.

II. The Pharisee
   A. The Pharisees were a Jewish group that began their ministry in the intertestamental period.
      i. The Pharisees were profoundly concerned about the decline in religion and the neglect in the law of God that they observed among the Jewish people at that time.
      ii. Amidst a secularizing culture, the Pharisees were committed to keeping God's law and upholding godliness among the people.
   B. Eventually, many Pharisees became more focused on their obedience to the law, rather than on what the law was originally designed to teach.
      i. The law of God is intended to reveal God's holiness and human sin.
      ii. God's law acts as a schoolmaster, driving fallen people to Christ as they realize that they cannot keep God's holy commandments. (Romans 7:7-8; Galatians 3:19; Galatians 3:24-25)
      iii. Rather than seeing their own sin in the mirror of the law, many Pharisees only saw their own moral effort and achievement.
      iv. Many sought to win God's approval by keeping themselves separate from any person or thing that was seen as polluted or unclean.

C. The Pharisee in this parable had the audacity to thank God for his perceived moral superiority over others.
   i. Though his words expressed gratitude for God's grace in his life, his prayer lacked sincerity.
   ii. His prayer adopted the tone of reminding God and others of his righteous lifestyle, in contrast to the dishonesty and corruption of others.
   iii. The Pharisee's words indicated that he thought his righteous works would help him to earn favor in God's eyes.

D. Sadly, many people have a mistaken understanding of what it takes to be justified before God.
   i. Many, like this Pharisee, still trust in their own achievements and good works to make them right with God.
   ii. Thinking that God grades us on a curve, we compare our behavior to others and assume God will accept us as long as there is someone else who is worse than us.
   iii. It is commonly thought that a person will go to heaven simply if his or her good deeds outweigh the bad deeds.

E. Yet, what God requires is perfection.
   i. If God kept a record of iniquities, no one could stand in His presence. (Psalm 130:3)
   ii. Even in our good deeds, we fail to love God with all our hearts, minds, and strength.
   iii. As depraved creatures, everything that we do is marred by the imperfection of the sinful heart and will performing the action.

III. The Tax Collector

A. In contrast to the haughty spirit of the Pharisee, the tax collector stood far off and would not even raise his eyes to heaven.

B. His demeanor was one of utter humility.

C. He understood the serious nature of his sin and expressed genuine sorrow over it.
   i. He recognized that he stood before a holy God empty-handed.
   ii. Rather than gloat about his own achievements, the tax collector simply cried out for mercy.

D. The tax collector, not the Pharisee, went away justified before God.

IV. The Imputation of Christ's Righteousness

A. The doctrine of imputation teaches that the justification that sinners receive before God is grounded in a righteousness that is not their own.
   i. By faith, sinners receive an "alien righteousness."
   ii. This "alien righteousness" comes from outside of us.

B. In order to reconcile fallen humanity to God, Jesus Christ did not simply arrive on earth and then die upon the cross.
   i. In His work of passive obedience, Christ died on the cross to pay the penalty for human sin.

   ii. In His work of active obedience, Christ lived a perfectly sinless life and earned the righteousness that God requires from every person.
   iii. When sinners trust in Christ alone, He imputes, or transfers, His righteous status to them.

C. In this parable, the tax collector rested on God's grace alone.
   i. In justification, God pronounces a person to be just who is not just in and of himself.
   ii. With this justifying pronouncement, God removes that person's guilt and grants him or her the dazzling and enduring righteousness of Christ.
   iii. When the tax collector went to his house justified, he walked away as a forgiven and adopted son of God.

STUDY QUESTIONS

1. To say that the church is outwardly a *corpus permixtum* is to say that it includes both true believers and those who have professed faith without actually possessing it.
   a. True
   b. False

2. In his prayer, the Pharisee focused on ___________.
   a. His need for forgiveness
   b. God's holiness
   c. His daily needs
   d. His obedience to God's laws

3. When the tax collector prayed, he ___________.
   a. Thanked God that he was not like the Pharisee
   b. Promised to give all he had to the poor
   c. Confessed his sin and begged God for mercy
   d. Raised his arms and lifted his eyes up to heaven

4. By faith, repentant sinners receive a righteousness that comes from deep within them.
   a. True
   b. False

5. In His ___________, Jesus Christ earned the righteousness that God requires from every person.
   a. Active obedience
   b. Passive obedience
   c. Atoning death
   d. Victory over death

BIBLE STUDY AND DISCUSSION QUESTIONS

1. How does the law of God act as a mirror? What did the Pharisee see when he looked at the mirror of God's law? What did the tax collector see?

2. What is right and true about the Pharisee's prayer? What is problematic? Based on this prayer, how did the Pharisee see himself before God?

3. Generally, what were the Pharisees like in Jesus' day? How were tax collectors regarded at this time? How do you think Jesus' listeners would have responded to the descriptions of the Pharisee and the tax collector in this parable?

4. In what ways are you tempted to behave like the Pharisee in this parable? Who are some "tax collectors" that you find it easy to look down upon? What might you be able to learn from these people about humility and true faith?

8

Parable of the Unforgiving Servant

MESSAGE INTRODUCTION

Life in a fallen world is all too often characterized by broken trust, strained relationships, and unmet expectations. Intentionally or not, we are constantly hurting others and being hurt by others. As a result, the parable of the unforgiving servant in Matthew 18 describes our need both to forgive others and to be forgiven by them. As we explore this parable, we will see how God's abundant forgiveness changes the way we live and relate to Him and to the people around us.

SCRIPTURE READINGS

Matthew 18:21-35

TEACHING OBJECTIVES

1. To present and exegete the parable of the unforgiving servant in Matthew 18:21-35.
2. To explain what forgiveness is and why we need God's forgiveness.
3. To promote a greater appreciation for God's mercy.
4. To encourage a lifestyle of forgiving others.

QUOTATIONS

Look how they will answer it another day, who, though they bear the Christian name, persist in the most rigorous and unmerciful treatment of their brethren, as if the strictest laws of Christ might be dispensed with for the gratifying of their unbridled passions; and so they curse themselves every time they say the Lord's prayer.

–Matthew Henry

We are not to limit our forgiveness to any fixed number of times. As often as a brother injures us, and asks forgiveness, we are to forgive him. It is his duty to ask forgiveness. If he does this, it is our duty to declare that we forgive him, and to treat him accordingly. If he does not ask us to forgive him, yet we are not at liberty to follow him with revenge and malice, but are still to treat him kindly, and to do him good.

–Albert Barnes

LECTURE OUTLINE

I. Forgiveness and Church Discipline
   A. Before telling the parable of the unforgiving servant in Matthew 18:21-35, Jesus gave instructions about responding to interpersonal sins in Matthew 18:15-20.
      i. If one Christian sins against another, the one who has been wronged is to confront the offender privately.
      ii. If the offender does not repent, the one who has been wronged is to confront him once more, accompanied by one or two other mature believers.
      iii. If the offender still refuses to listen, the matter is to be brought before the church.
      iv. If the offender remains unrepentant and does not listen to the church, he is to be regarded as an unbeliever.
   B. One of the most difficult experiences for the community of believers is confronting a church member who refuses to repent of sin.
      i. This process of confrontation is commonly referred to as church discipline.
      ii. The goal of this process is not to punish the offending brother, but to bring him to repentance and restoration within the church.
      iii. Impenitence for sin is the only biblical grounds for excommunicating a person from the church.
      iv. Even after excommunication, Christians should still hope to see this person eventually restored to faithful discipleship within the body of Christ.
   C. When Peter asked about forgiveness after Jesus gave these instructions, Peter was in effect asking how many times he should be willing to confront in this way a brother who had wronged him.
      i. If a brother sins against Peter, Peter confronts the brother, and the brother then repents, how many times should Peter confront the brother if the same offense happens again?
      ii. Jesus responded that Peter should be prepared to forgive a person as many times as it takes.
   D. Forgiveness is a weighty pronouncement.
      i. When God forgives someone, He no longer holds that sin against the person.
      ii. Though God does not keep a record of the wrongs He has forgiven, we often do.

iii. When we keep a scorecard of sins committed against us, we demonstrate that we have not truly forgiven those who have sinned against us.
iv. When Peter suggested that he keep a scorecard of seven sins, Jesus reminded him that true forgiveness does not keep a scorecard.

II. The King's Act of Forgiveness
A. This parable begins with a king settling accounts with his servants.
B. One of the servants owed the king 10,000 talents.
i. Even a single talent was an extraordinary sum of money, the highest monetary unit in that day.
ii. A talent was the equivalent of many years' wages.
iii. 10,000 talents would have been over ten times the amount of King Herod's annual revenue.
iv. Such a debt was too large for any servant of any king in the ancient world to repay.
C. It is striking that Jesus compares his disciples to this debtor.
i. Every time that a person breaks God's law, he or she becomes a debtor.
ii. Each person has incurred a moral debt to God that is virtually infinite.
iii. Like the servant in the parable, we are unable to repay our immense spiritual debts.
D. Because of his great debt, all that the servant could do was beg the king for a second chance to pay what he owed.
i. Yet, even if the king had demonstrated infinite patience, infinity would not be long enough for the servant to repay the debt.
ii. Although he could not fathom the full extent of his debt, he recognized that his only hope would be to receive the king's compassion.
E. The king's kindness and compassion exceeded the servant's expectations.
i. The servant fell to his knees and begged the king to give him more time.
ii. Instead of giving the servant more time to repay his debt, the king released him from the debt completely.
iii. The king did not just forgive the servant a portion of the debt, but he forgave him every cent that he owed.
F. Because of the king's kindness, the servant and his family were spared from being sold into slavery, and he was freed from the burden of having to raise such a vast sum of money.

III. The Servant's Lack of Forgiveness
A. As he departed, the forgiven servant met one of his fellow servants who owed him one hundred denarii.
i. The denarius was a smaller monetary unit, and it took thousands of denarii to equal a single talent.
ii. This debt, which could have been repaid in a matter of weeks, was nothing compared to the first servant's debt, which never could have been repaid.

B. The forgiven servant seized the other servant, demanded payment, and had him thrown into debtor's prison.
    i. Although the second servant begged for mercy in the same way that the first servant had, the first servant refused to forgive him his small debt.
    ii. Sadly, the servant who had been forgiven failed to pass along even a tiny portion of the compassion that he had received.

C. When the other servants told the king what had happened, he summoned the servant and delivered him to the jailers until he could pay his debt in full.
    i. The servant had been threatened with justice, but had instead received mercy.
    ii. When he despised the mercy and grace of the king, he received justice.
    iii. In the same way, when forgiven sinners refuse to be conduits of the grace that has saved us, we can expect to receive nothing less than justice from God.

IV. Forgiveness and the Christian Life

A. Christians often say that the Bible requires unilateral forgiveness.
    i. This would mean that Christians must forgive all who sin against them, whether they repent or not.
    ii. Christians have the right to forgive others unilaterally without requiring repentance.
    iii. This is what Jesus did when He asked the Father to forgive His tormenters when they did not realize the severity of their sinful actions.

B. We may extend this kind of unilateral forgiveness if we choose, but it is technically not required.
    i. The Bible typically mentions repentance as a prerequisite to forgiveness.
    ii. Scripture does not actually demand forgiveness where repentance is absent.
    iii. If Christians were required to forgive the unrepentant, the process of discipline in Matthew 18:15-20 would be irrelevant.

C. What God does require is complete forgiveness of those who have repented of their sins.
    i. If one Christian confronts another about his sin, and if he repents, the one who has been wronged must extend forgiveness to the repentant offender.
    ii. We must stand willing and ready to forgive any insult or offense that anyone has ever committed against us if that person repents of the sin.

D. God calls His people to demonstrate a forgiving spirit.
    i. Holding grudges or harboring bitterness can be extremely destructive.
    ii. Jesus urged His followers to ask God to forgive our debts as we forgive our debtors.
    iii. Unless we are willing to forgive those who sin against us, we should not expect God to forgive us when we sin against Him.

iv. Since God's extravagant forgiveness toward us is at the heart of the Christian faith, we should be known as a forgiving people.

STUDY QUESTIONS

1. According to Matthew 18, ___________ is cause for being excommunicated from the church.
   a. A theological disagreement
   b. Missing a worship service
   c. Insulting the pastor
   d. Impenitence for sin

2. How much money did the servant owe the king?
   a. More than he could ever repay
   b. 100 denarii
   c. 100 talents
   d. 1,000 talents

3. The servant who had been forgiven failed to extend forgiveness to others.
   a. True
   b. False

4. At the end of the parable, the servant who owed the king a large sum of money received ___________.
   a. Mercy
   b. Justice
   c. Grace
   d. Unjust punishment

5. The Bible requires Christians to forgive others unconditionally, whether they express repentance or not.
   a. True
   b. False

BIBLE STUDY AND DISCUSSION QUESTIONS

1. How do Jesus' instructions in Matthew 18:15-20 influence your understanding of the parable in Matthew 18:21-35?

2. What does this parable say about your condition before God? Describe the spiritual debt that you owe to God. How has God handled this debt?

3. How does an awareness of the extent of your own sin affect the way that you regard other people's sins against you? How does God's forgiveness of your sins change the way that you relate to other people?

4. When do you find it most difficult to forgive someone? What kinds of requirements and conditions do you wait for people to meet before you forgive them? Have you been withholding forgiveness from someone who has sinned against you?

9

Parable of the Good Samaritan

MESSAGE INTRODUCTION

As we consider God's holy ways and His desires for us, we sadly tend to limit our obedience according to what comes most easily to us. When we are commanded to love our neighbor as ourself, for instance, we tend to seek out people that are like us and that are easy for us to love. In this lecture, we will examine the parable of the Good Samaritan, a well-known passage that conveys a biblical understanding of what it truly means to love one's neighbor.

SCRIPTURE READINGS

Luke 10:25-37

TEACHING OBJECTIVES

1. To present and exegete the parable of the Good Samaritan in Luke 10:25-37.
2. To describe the uneasy relationship between Jews and Samaritans.
3. To discuss the biblical idea of neighbor.
4. To encourage Christians to be active in helping others who are in need.

QUOTATIONS

Brothers and sisters, let what we do for others always be done in the noblest style! Let us not treat the poor like dogs to whom we fling a bone, nor visit the sick like superior beings who feel that they are stooping down to inferiors when they enter their rooms. But in the sweet tenderness of real love, learned at Jesus' feet, let us imitate this Good Samaritan!

–Charles Spurgeon

For the love Jesus demands is love of one's neighbor, that is to say, not some general love of mankind, but a love that does not pick and choose, that is unreservedly and principally committed to God's will and guidance also with respect to its object. For the neighbor is anyone whom God places in our way, as is described in such an unparalleled and beautiful way in the parable of the Good Samaritan.

–Herman Ridderbos

LECTURE OUTLINE

I. Jesus and the Lawyer
  A. A lawyer asked Jesus how he could obtain eternal life.
    i. Unfortunately, this man was not genuinely seeking wisdom.
    ii. His underlying motive was to put Jesus to the test.
  B. Since this man was an expert in the law, Jesus asked him what the law taught.
    i. Jesus tried to help others truly understand the law.
    ii. By understanding the law, they would realize the futility of trying to work their way into heaven.
  C. When Jesus told him to obey the law by loving God and neighbor, the man asked him, "Who is my neighbor?"
    i. This was likely an escape mechanism.
    ii. First-century Jewish culture defined being a neighbor narrowly, including only fellow Jews who lived righteously.

II. Jews and Samaritans
  A. First-century Jews would not have considered Samaritans to be neighbors.
  B. Though geographically close, Samaritans were culturally and religiously distant from Jews.
  C. The enmity between these communities had existed for centuries.
    i. When the inhabitants of Israel had been taken into captivity by the Assyrians, the area was resettled by foreigners who intermarried with the remaining locals.
    ii. In this setting, worship of the true God blended with pagan practices. (2 Kings 17:24-41)
    iii. The Samaritans worshipped at a temple on Mount Gerizim instead of at the Jerusalem temple.
    iv. When the inhabitants of Judah returned from exile in Babylon, they experienced opposition and antagonism from the Samaritans.
  D. In the first century, Jews avoided interacting with the Samaritans.
  E. When Jesus travelled through Samaria (John 4:1-44), conscientious Jews would have been shocked that He willingly passed through that region instead of going around it.

III. The Good Samaritan

A. The parable begins with a man travelling from Jerusalem to Jericho.
   i. These two cities were separated by seventeen miles of desolate countryside.
   ii. Merchants would often travel this road in order to sell their wares in Jericho.
   iii. The desolate and rocky terrain made this road a popular site for bandit raids.
B. On the way, this man was attacked by thieves, who wounded him, stripped him of his belongings, and left him there to die.
C. A priest passed by the injured man but refused to help him.
   i. The priest saw this man and walked by on the other side of the road.
   ii. The priest did not know whether the victim was dead or alive.
   iii. If the priest touched a corpse, he would have needed to undergo cleansing rituals in order to resume his priestly duties.
   iv. Rather than risk having to go through the purification rituals, the priest stayed away from the injured man.
D. A Levite also walked by and refused to help the dying man.
   i. As a member of the consecrated tribe, this man had been set apart to teach and do the work of God.
   ii. Though this man's vocation included doing deeds of mercy, he was willing to let the injured man perish alone and unaided.
E. A Samaritan came upon the victim and did not ignore him.
   i. The Samaritan had compassion upon the dying man.
   ii. The Samaritan's compassion led him to action.
   iii. He bandaged the man's wounds, anointed the man with oil and wine, and placed him upon his own horse.
   iv. The Samaritan paused his journey, took the injured man to an inn, and spent the rest of the day taking care of him.
   v. When the Samaritan left the next day, he made arrangements to pay for the wounded man's expenses.

IV. Who is My Neighbor?

A. Of the three passers-by, the Samaritan was the only one who showed himself to be a neighbor to the injured man.
   i. This parable does not simply exhort us to have compassion upon those who are in need.
   ii. This parable answers the question "Who is my neighbor?" by demonstrating that there are not ethnic or geographical limits to the kingdom of God.
B. Though the Bible denies universal brotherhood, it affirms universal neighborhood.
   i. Every human being created in the image of God is a neighbor.
   ii. Christians are called to love every human being on earth as much as we love ourselves.

   iii. Even if a person is not a part of the household of faith, that person is still a Christian's neighbor.

C. The Christian's task is not to condemn those who have fallen into the gutter, but to help them out of the gutter.

D. After showing this picture of mercy, Jesus bids His listeners to "go and do likewise."

STUDY QUESTIONS

1. The Jews disliked the Samaritans for all the following reasons except ___________.
   a. The Samaritans had harassed the Jews who returned from exile.
   b. The Samaritans did not worship at the temple in Jerusalem.
   c. The Samaritans formed a military alliance with Rome.
   d. The Samaritans had blended true worship with paganism.

2. If the priest or Levite had stopped to help the dying man, they would have run the risk of becoming ceremonially unclean.
   a. True
   b. False

3. How did the Samaritan respond to the injured man?
   a. Like the priest and Levite before him, he ignored the injured man.
   b. He treated his wounds, took him to an inn, and paid his expenses.
   c. He did not stop for long, but he gave the man some food and water.
   d. He took the man into his home and made him part of his family.

4. All three travelers were neighbors to the robbed and injured man, but only the Samaritan was a friend to him.
   a. True
   b. False

5. The Bible teaches the universal ___________ of all people.
   a. Brotherhood
   b. Neighborhood
   c. Parenthood
   d. Sonship

BIBLE STUDY AND DISCUSSION QUESTIONS

1. What did the lawyer ask Jesus? Based on the lawyer's words, how did he understand God's law?

2. Why is it significant that Jesus responded to the lawyer's questions by telling this parable? How do you think the lawyer would have reacted to this parable?

3. Why do you think the priest and the Levite did not stop to help the dying man? Are these good reasons? When you see someone in trouble, what is your first instinct? Why do you respond this way?

4. How did Jesus' definition of a neighbor differ from the lawyer's idea of a neighbor? How do Jesus' words challenge your own way of thinking about who your neighbors are?

10

Parable of the Prodigal Son

MESSAGE INTRODUCTION

Out of all the parables of Jesus, one of the most well-known is the story of a son who broke his father's heart by demanding an early inheritance and running away from home. Finally realizing the folly of his ways and the emptiness of the life he had chosen, the young man returned home and was welcomed by his father with joyous celebration. This is a powerful story in its own right, but it also illustrates profound spiritual truths. As we turn our attention to this parable, we will be reminded of both the gravity of human sin and God's joy every time a sinner seeks forgiveness and refuge in His fatherly arms.

SCRIPTURE READINGS

Luke 15:1-3, 11-32

TEACHING OBJECTIVES

1. To present and exegete the parable of the prodigal son in Luke 15:11-32.
2. To describe the tragic consequences of human rebellion against God.
3. To celebrate the unconditional and forgiving love of God.
4. To promote a deep sense of joy for the salvation of each sinner who turns to Jesus Christ for forgiveness and newness of life.

QUOTATIONS

If men, who are by nature prone to revenge, and too tenacious of their own rights, are moved by fatherly love kindly to forgive their children, and freely to bring them back, when they are sunk in wretchedness, God, whose boundless goodness exceeds all the affection of parents, will not treat us more harshly. And certainly nothing is here attributed to an earthly father which God does not promise with respect to himself. "Before they call," says he, "I will answer."

–John Calvin

Nowhere have the concepts of sin, repentance, and divine grace been depicted more vividly and impressively than in the parable of the prodigal son; sin—as leaving the fellowship of the father, in living far away from the father, in the wasting of the father's goods; repentance—in the discovery of his own distress, in his consciousness of having sinned against the father and having lost all the rights of a child, in his return to the father; grace—in the father's awaiting of the son, in his pity for him, and in the joyful reception of the lost son into the father's house.

–Herman Ridderbos

LECTURE OUTLINE

I. A Lost Son
  - A. A man had two sons, and the younger son asked the father to give him his inheritance early.
    - i. This was a highly offensive demand to make.
    - ii. Nevertheless, the father divided his property and gave the younger son his inheritance.
  - B. The younger son then gathered all that he had, left home, went to a distant country, and embraced a reckless lifestyle.
    - i. Rather than live riotously at home, he moved far away.
    - ii. When young people rebel, they tend to leave their inhibitions, familial ties, and cultural taboos back where they came from.
    - iii. By going to a distant land, this son went to a place where no one from home could see him, critique his lifestyle, or stop him.
  - C. The son squandered his entire inheritance.
    - i. His prodigal lifestyle cost him everything he had.
    - ii. He wasted the gift of wealth that his father had given him.

II. An Awakened Son
  - A. After the son spent all his money, a severe famine came upon the land.
  - B. With no resources to fall back on, the son was compelled to earn a living by taking care of pigs.
    - i. In Jewish culture, pigs were considered to be unclean animals.
    - ii. Serving as a caretaker to pigs represented utter humiliation.
  - C. The young man was so hungry that he would have gladly eaten the food that he was feeding to the pigs.
  - D. Finally, the son "came to himself" and realized the severity of his situation. (Luke 15:17)

i. At certain times, God awakes people to their spiritual danger.
ii. This happened on a large scale in the eighteenth-century revival known as the Great Awakening.
iii. In situations like these, people awaken from their unconscious life of sin, their consciences are aroused, and they seek God's forgiveness.
iv. Similarly, the son came to his senses, realized that his situation was hopeless, and decided to seek his father's forgiveness.

III. A Forgiving Father

A. The repentant son made the return journey to his father's home.
   i. He planned to confess his sin to his father.
   ii. No longer worthy to be called a son, he hoped to be hired as a servant in his father's household.
B. The father saw his son approaching in the distance, recognized him, and went out to meet him.
   i. Not content to walk, the father ran toward his son.
   ii. In the ancient world, men wore long robes that made running difficult and undignified.
C. The father forgave and restored his son.
   i. He embraced his son and kissed him.
   ii. Instead of rebuking his son, he showered him with fatherly love.
   iii. He summoned the servants to bring him fine clothes that were fit for a son.
D. The father held a lavish celebration.
   i. The household feasted upon the fattened calf.
   ii. They celebrated with music and dancing.
   iii. The son had been dead, but was now alive.
   iv. The son had been lost, but now was found.

IV. A Hard-Hearted Brother

A. As the older brother returned from the field, he heard the sound of music and dancing.
B. The brother became angry and refused to join the celebration.
   i. Although he had served his father faithfully for many years, he complained that he had never been given even a young goat to enjoy with his friends.
   ii. He was outraged that his brother—who had left and squandered the family's wealth—received a warm homecoming celebration.
   iii. Sadly, the older brother did not truly understand grace.
   iv. Like the Pharisees in Jesus' day, the older brother was more concerned with being rewarded for his righteous deed than with the salvation of "tax collectors and sinners." (Luke 15:1)

C. The father reminded the brother of the significance of what had taken place.
   i. The older brother had been with the father always, and his inheritance remained secure.
   ii. On the other hand, the younger brother was dead but is now alive; though once lost, he has now been found.
   iii. Those who truly understand grace cannot help but rejoice when a sinner receives forgiveness and mercy from God.

STUDY QUESTIONS

1. What did the younger son do with his inheritance money?
   a. He squandered his money on wild living.
   b. He built a lavish home.
   c. He purchased land and rented it out to dishonest tenants.
   d. He made foolish speculative investments.

2. What happened to the younger son when the famine came?
   a. He immediately returned home.
   b. He was able to get by on the money that he had saved.
   c. He began taking care of pigs as a hired hand.
   d. His new friends took care of him.

3. When the younger son returned to his father's home, his hope was that his father would permit him to work as a servant.
   a. True
   b. False

4. The father received his younger son by ___________.
   a. Scolding him for his rebellion and folly
   b. Sending the older brother to slaughter the fattened calf
   c. Running toward him and embracing him
   d. Accepting his offer to work as a servant

5. The older brother joined in the celebration despite his apathy about the younger brother's return.
   a. True
   b. False

BIBLE STUDY AND DISCUSSION QUESTIONS

1. How does the background information in Luke 15:1-3 help us understand the parables of the lost sheep, the lost coin, and the lost son?

2. Dr. Sproul observed that, just as the prodigal son wasted his father's inheritance, we often waste or misuse the good gifts that God has given us. What are some ways that you have done this? When we waste these gifts, what does this indicate about our relationship with God?

3. What did it take to bring the young man to his senses? How has God acted in your life to get your attention and draw you toward Him?

4. How did the older brother respond to the celebration when the younger brother returned? How was his attitude like that of the scribes and the Pharisees? In what ways do Christians continue to behave like the older brother today?

11

Parable of the Ten Virgins

MESSAGE INTRODUCTION

As a common adage reminds us, things are not always as they seem. It would be comforting to think that all of those who profess faith in Jesus Christ—all who outwardly worship Him, perform acts of service in His Name, and tell others about Him—will one day share in His victory. Sadly, however, this is not the case. The parable of the ten virgins, one of the most tragic and sobering of Jesus' parables, reminds us that not all who profess faith in Jesus truly know Him. We must take heed of this warning and find shelter in Christ, so that we will be prepared to meet Him when He returns or calls us to His side.

SCRIPTURE READINGS

Matthew 25:1-13

TEACHING OBJECTIVES

1. To present and exegete the parable of the ten virgins in Matthew 25:1-13.
2. To describe the importance of being prepared for the return of Christ.
3. To echo the biblical warning that not all professing Christians are truly ready to meet the Lord.
4. To encourage genuine, prayerful introspection about the state of one's soul before God.

QUOTATIONS

Our great duty is to watch, to attend to the business of our souls with the utmost diligence and circumspection. Be awake, and be wakeful. It is a good reason for our watching, that the time of our Lord's coming is very uncertain; we know neither the day nor the hour. Therefore every day and every hour we must be ready, and not off our watch any day in the year, or any hour in the day. Be thou in the fear of the Lord every day and all the day long.

–Matthew Henry

You must be justified in Christ's righteousness and you must put on His wedding dress, or else you will not be ready. You must be reconciled to God. You must be made like God or you will not be ready. Or, to come to the parable before us, you must have a lamp—and that lamp must be fed with heavenly oil—and it must continue to burn brightly, or else you will not be ready. No child of darkness can go into that place of God's Light! You must be brought out of nature's darkness into God's marvelous Light, or else you will never be ready to go in with Christ to the marriage and to be forever with Him.

–Charles Spurgeon

LECTURE OUTLINE

I. Lamps Without Oil
   A. In first-century Palestine, one would typically use a small lamp to lighten the way after dark.
      i. The lamps that were used were flat clay structures that were held in the palm of a hand.
      ii. The lamps included an empty space that would hold oil, and separate containers would often contain oil reserves.
      iii. A wick was situated at the top of the lamp, and it depended on oil to fuel the flame when it was ignited.
   B. A lamp without oil would be as useless as a modern electric lamp or flashlight without a light bulb.

II. Ten Bridesmaids
   A. The wedding refers to the second coming of Jesus Christ, the heavenly bridegroom, to be united with His bride, the church.
   B. The ten virgins in this parable were invited to the wedding to serve as bridesmaids.
      i. The bride had personally invited them to serve as her ladies in waiting.
      ii. These virgins would help to prepare the bride for the glorious moment of marriage.
      iii. As part of the inner circle, they held an honored status.
   C. Five of the bridesmaids were wise, and the other five were foolish and came to the wedding unprepared.
      i. This is a disconcerting reminder that, even among the inner circle, there are some who do not truly belong.
      ii. The foolish bridesmaids represent professing Christians who are part of the visible church but do not truly know the Lord.

III. A Lack of Oil

A. Because the groom did not arrive at the expected time, the wedding was delayed for several hours.
   i. As they waited, the bridesmaids fell asleep.
   ii. Around midnight, they were alerted that the bridegroom was on his way.
   iii. They began to trim their lamps and prepare for the groom's arrival.

B. The wise virgins had brought an adequate supply of oil to keep their lamps burning, but the foolish virgins had not.

C. Since oil is what distinguishes the wise bridesmaids from the foolish ones, there have been various views throughout church history about what the oil represents.
   i. Many Roman Catholics have identified the oil with good works.
   ii. Many Protestants have identified the oil with the Holy Spirit.

IV. The Arrival of the Bridegroom

A. The wise bridesmaids did not have enough oil to share with the foolish bridesmaids.

B. The foolish virgins followed the advice of the wise and went out to purchase additional oil.

C. While they were gone, however, the bridegroom arrived.
   i. When the bridegroom came, the wedding party entered the building where the wedding was to take place.
   ii. As was the custom, the doors to the building were shut and locked once the wedding party had entered.

D. The five foolish bridesmaids returned to the site of the wedding to find that the door had already been shut.

E. They begged the groom to open the door, crying out, "Lord, Lord!"
   i. In the Bible, the repetition of a name often communicates intimacy, such as "Abram, Abram!" and "Absalom, Absalom!"
   ii. The bridesmaids appealed to an intimate knowledge of the groom.
   iii. Yet, the bridegroom replied that he did not know them.

V. A Solemn Warning

A. As Jesus cautioned in Matthew 7:21, "Not everyone who says to me, 'Lord, Lord,' will enter the kingdom of heaven, but the one who does the will of my Father who is in heaven."
   i. Some will say, "Lord, Lord, did we not prophesy in your name?"
   ii. Others will say, "Did we not cast out demons in your name and do mighty works in your name?"
   iii. Yet, Jesus will declare, "I never knew you; depart from me, you workers of lawlessness." (Matthew 7:23)

B. When Jesus says, "I never knew you," He is not speaking in a cognitive sense, but in a personal, filial, and redemptive sense: "I never knew you savingly."

C. The oil that the five bridesmaids lacked is saving faith.
    i. This parable is not speaking about pagans who have never heard the gospel.
    ii. Rather, it speaks of the danger awaiting those who profess faith in Christ without actually possessing it.

D. It is not yet too late to repent and believe in the Lord Jesus.
    i. Tragically, there are many in the church today who do not truly know Jesus Christ.
    ii. Everyone who makes a profession of faith is invited to the wedding feast of the Lamb, but not all will attend.
    iii. This parable calls all professing Christians to examine themselves prayerfully to discern whether they truly have saving faith.

STUDY QUESTIONS

1. What role were the five foolish virgins intended to play in the wedding?
    a. They were there mainly to provide light for the guests.
    b. They were guests who did not know the bride or groom well.
    c. They were part of the bride's inner circle.
    d. None; they were crashing the wedding.

2. The wise virgins brought enough oil for their lamps, but the foolish virgins did not bring any oil.
    a. True
    b. False

3. What happened when the foolish virgins needed oil for their lamps?
    a. They entered the wedding feast without oil.
    b. They went away to buy oil.
    c. The wise virgins gave them oil.
    d. They decided to go back to their homes.

4. In the Bible, the repetition of a name or title often expresses ___________.
    a. Fear
    b. Anger
    c. Urgency
    d. Intimacy

5. According to Dr. Sproul, the oil in the parable represents righteous deeds.
    a. True
    b. False

BIBLE STUDY AND DISCUSSION QUESTIONS

1. Some of the bridesmaids were not prepared to wait the full measure of time before the bridegroom's arrival. Similarly, Christ has not returned to earth as quickly as many early Christians supposed that He would. What are some of the advantages of this present waiting period for the church? What challenges or dangers does this waiting period present for Christians?

2. Why is it significant that half of the bridesmaids were not able to join in the wedding feast? What does this fact indicate about the people who belong to the visible church? Why does Christ say that He has not known certain people who profess faith in Him and perform acts of service in His name?

3. What does the oil in this parable represent? How does having a full supply of this oil help Christians to await and persevere until the arrival of Jesus Christ? In what ways can a person's lack of oil cause their lamp to falter and flicker out before Jesus comes?

4. How do you respond to Jesus' statement that many who cry out, "Lord, Lord!" are not actually known by Him? What are some biblical ways that you can know whether you have saving faith?

12

Parable of the Talents

MESSAGE INTRODUCTION

As Psalm 24:1 proclaims, "The earth is the LORD's, and everything in it, the world, and all who live in it." Amidst a culture that exalts consumerism and human autonomy, these words remind us that we and everything we own belong to God. This reality has far-reaching implications for how we manage our time, abilities, relationships, finances, and Christian witness. In our study of the parable of the talents, we shall see that, as followers of Jesus Christ, it is both our responsibility and our privilege to utilize the resources under our care for the glory of God and the growth of His church.

SCRIPTURE READINGS

Matthew 25:14-30

TEACHING OBJECTIVES

1. To present and exegete the parable of the talents in Matthew 25:14-30.
2. To describe the biblical concept of stewardship.
3. To emphasize each Christian's responsibility to participate in the mission of the church.
4. To evoke a longing to hear Christ one day say the words, "Well done, good and faithful servant."

QUOTATIONS

Whatever abilities and advantages we have, they are not our own; we are but stewards of them, and must give account to our Lord, whose goods they are.

–Matthew Henry

Men of slender abilities may often do more good in the world than men of much greater talents. It is rather a warm heart than a strong head which is required to do good. A humble Christian, by his life, example, and conversation, may often do much more good than is done by those in more elevated stations, and with far greater gifts.

–Albert Barnes

LECTURE OUTLINE

I. Biblical Stewardship
   A. As a wealthy man prepared to depart on a long journey, he placed talents under the stewardship of three servants.
      i. In this case, a talent does not refer to a gift or ability.
      ii. Rather, a talent was the highest unit of currency used by the Jews at that time.
   B. The master distributed the talents to the servants according to his perception of their ability to use money productively.
      i. One servant received five talents, another servant received two talents, and a third servant received one talent.
      ii. These servants were entrusted with considerable sums of money, exceeding several years' worth of wages.
   C. This parable relates to the biblical concept of stewardship.
      i. Many people see in this parable a biblical case for capitalism, but the purpose of this parable is not to promote any particular economic system.
      ii. Rather, this parable acknowledges the wisdom of investing resources wisely and productively.
      iii. In the ancient world, stewards were appointed to manage the finances and administrative workings of a household.
      iv. The Greek term *oikonomia*, meaning "house rule," is the root of the English words "economy" and "economics."
      v. Though a steward did not own the property, he was responsible for managing it well.
      vi. Similarly, Christians acknowledge that God owns all things and we are to manage faithfully all the resources, opportunities, and abilities that He has entrusted to us.

II. Productivity and the Christian Life
   A. The doctrine of justification by faith should not become an excuse for poor stewardship of God's gifts.
      i. Many Christians believe that, because we are not saved by our works, if a person has a warm, loving heart there is no need to work as a Christian.
      ii. The New Testament's emphasis on spiritual fruit is a reminder that God expects believers to put their faith into action.

B. Historically, the Reformation tradition has emphasized the responsibilities of individual Christians.
   i. When Martin Luther articulated the concept of the priesthood of all believers, he reminded ordinary Christians that God has given them work to do.
   ii. Part of the role of the clergy is to equip lay people for ministry.
   iii. Christians have different spiritual gifts, but they all have a responsibility to participate in the mission of the church.

C. One day we will be called upon to give an account to God of how we have used the things that He has given us.
   i. Like the servants in this parable, we will need to give an account for our stewardship of His money.
   ii. We will also need to account for our stewardship of time, resources, abilities, and everything else that He has entrusted to us.

III. The Master's Return

A. When the master returned to settle accounts with his servants, the first two servants had doubled the number of talents in their possession.
   i. The servant who had been given five talents had invested, traded, and gained an additional five talents.
   ii. The servant who had been given two talents had gained an additional two talents.
   iii. The master responded, "Well done, good and faithful servant."
   iv. Because these servants had been faithful with little, they would now be trusted with greater things.
   v. The master invited them to enter into his joy.

B. The third servant, however, had not used his talent well.
   i. He said that he had been afraid of his master, and he falsely accused the master of dishonesty.
   ii. Rather than risk losing his single talent, he had buried it in the ground.
   iii. He simply returned to the master the exact sum that he had been given.
   iv. The master responded, "You wicked and slothful servant!"
   v. The master took the talent away from this servant and gave it to the servant with ten talents.

C. Whoever has produced much will be given more.

D. Whoever has not produced anything will lose everything.

E. Apart from God's grace, we are all unprofitable servants.
   i. Left to our own devices, we squander God's good gifts.
   ii. In Christ, we become new creatures and can share faithfully in the work He has given us to do.
   iii. As our faith bears fruit in our lives, we long for the day when we shall hear the Father say, "Well done, good and faithful servant."

STUDY QUESTIONS

1. In the context of Matthew 25:14-30, a talent refers to ___________.
   a. A spiritual gift.
   b. A unit of currency.
   c. A unique ability or skill.
   d. All of the above.

2. When the master entrusted talents to his servants, he distributed them based on his perception of each servant's stewardship capacity.
   a. True
   b. False

3. Which English word comes from the Greek word *oikonomia*?
   a. Administration.
   b. Iconography.
   c. Homemaking.
   d. Economy.

4. Because justification is not by works, God does not expect Christians to labor diligently in His service.
   a. True
   b. False

5. Which of the following is not true of the first two servants?
   a. They were commended for a job well done.
   b. They had each earned five talents.
   c. They were welcomed into the master's joy.
   d. They were given stewardship over more.

BIBLE STUDY AND DISCUSSION QUESTIONS

1. As Dr. Sproul indicated, in our familiarity with the gospel of grace we can sometimes develop an overly casual attitude toward God's holy character and His desires for us. How might our behavior reveal an underlying mindset of entitlement with regard to grace?

2. Biblically speaking, what does it mean to be a steward? In addition to this parable, what other examples of good stewardship are found in Scripture?

3. What are some of the abilities, resources, passions, and objects that God has entrusted to you? What are some ways that you can steward these gifts well?

4. In part, the reason that the third servant did not use his master's gift well was because he did not truly know or understand the character of his master. How can our fear, lack of faith, or misunderstanding of who God is lead us to misuse or squander the gifts that God has given to us?